HOW GREAT THOU ART

So Far So Glorious

FANELLA CHRISTIANA
SAMPSON

ISBN: 9798613024063

ACKNOWLEDGEMENTS

I take this opportunity to give thanks to God Almighty for enabling me to share my testimony of His goodness and faithfulness in my life.

To my daughters, Estella, Osmunda, and Minella, thanks for all your support in helping me write this book.

To my friend and sister Ramzeye Mustapha (Kamara), thank you for your continuous support throughout the years, in the good and bad times.

To my sisters Elizabeth and Hannah, thanks for the trip down memory lane as you both helped me remember the past.

To Apostle Kevin Etta and Pastor Imma Etta you have been an inspiration in my life, my children, and grandchildren's lives. I'm always thankful to God because He connected you and your family into our lives at the right time. Thanks for all that you have done for my family; may God richly bless you.

DEDICATION

To my dearly departed grandparents who did their best
to give me a bright future. They instilled in me the
belief that our present situation is not permanent and
that there will always be a better tomorrow.
Until we meet again.

CONTENTS

FOREWORD

By Ramzeye Kamara and Pastor Wonder Abodakpi

Ramzeye Kamara

In 1978, my husband was blessed with a job with the World Health Organization (WHO), through the U.N. So, my family was posted to Monrovia, Liberia.

My husband was assigned to the A.M. Dogliotti Medical School as a Medical Officer, lecturing in Anatomy and Physiology. While in Monrovia, I was fortunate to be employed by the University of Liberia, as an Instructor in the Teacher's College. I lectured at the University Teachers' College from 1978 to 1990, just before the onset of the Liberian Civil War that dilapidated the country.

I relocated to Minneapolis in 1990 only to hear from Fanella that she was in Oklahoma. Back in Liberia, we were fortunate to connect and become networked through schoolmates and classmates of my husband. In that comradeship, I was lucky to have come across Fanella Bangura. Fanella's family and mine became inextricably intertwined; hence a lifetime friendship was born.

Fanella mothered my oldest daughter, BK when she

attended her first year of secondary school in Freetown. Fanella is a very loving and caring person. She was sort of a mother to all the children in her neighborhood in Freetown. Due to the Civil wars both in Sierra Leone and Liberia, we were all displaced and for a long while no one knew the whereabouts of families and friends.

As per the Divine GPS of God our Father, Fanella and I reconnected again in the U.S. Since our divine reunion, our friendship has been blessed with the joys of God's benevolence and mercy. Our friendship is built on the solid rock of Christ with no regrets. She is my confidant and 'goto' person; very dependable, responsible and trusting. We have gone through thick and thin, through joys and sorrows. It was designed that Fanella and I would build a lifetime friendship and become true sisters in Christ. Our friendship has developed and evolved even deeper into a model of an ultra-tested and tried, trusting, respectable, dependable and all-weather type of friendship.

As lifetime friends, I would describe Fanella as a symbol of Biblical Ruth. She is indeed a type of Ruth. Fanella is a woman of loyalty and devotion. She is indeed a survivor of many sicknesses, hardships, disappointments and has gracefully endured all the trials and tribulations of life. She is a very courageous woman. In the face of daunting and sometimes overwhelming challenges and difficulties, she was able to prevail and by the grace of God raise three beautiful girls. She never wallows in her sorrows but overcomes them with courage. She is a very strong, diligent and capable woman of strong faith in God and is ever a lover of her Lord and Master Jesus Christ.

Fanella is very relaxed and easy-going but also very precautious. Fanella knows when it is time to play and when it is time to work. She can be a social bug and is very likeable. She is a very calm and cool-headed person. She has the faith of Abraham, never giving up in life. She is very faith-filled. Very compassionate and giving. She would always sympathize with the marginalized and is always eager to ease the pains of others. She never picks a fight with anyone. I always admired her glamour, and correctness. Sometimes she is perfect to a fault. She is very organized.

Fanella will always only ever give her best. In spite of all the challenges that beset her, Fanella successfully raised three beautiful girls in the house of God. She never wavered on how to raise her children, for in all Fanella does, God is first in her life. Fanella is a true example of letting go and letting God. She is a blessing to everyone that crosses her path. She has sacrificed her life not only for her marriages, and her children and the church but for all whom she encounters. I am blessed and highly favored to have such a stable, committed, dependable, trusting, joyful and godly woman as my friend. I consider myself extremely blessed by knowing this exceptional woman of faith and virtue.

It is my fervent belief that all who read this book will come to know Fanella, perhaps not in quite the way that I have known her, but enough to give God the glory for her extraordinary life, and be themselves drawn into the practice of a deeper fellowship and faith in God our Creator and His Son Jesus Christ our Lord.

Ramzeye Kamara, Minneapolis MN

* * *

Pastor Wonder Abodakpi

Everyone can attest to the fact that challenges are a constant part of life. You cannot avoid them or pay your way out of them. Even those for whom life seems to be a bed of roses, can admittedly attest to the fact that they have to learn to deal with the challenges of discomfort created by the thorns in the roses. It is said that you can either complain that roses have thorns or be thankful that thorns have roses. It's all a matter of perspective and one's level of faith. Life is a gift but more than that, it is a responsibility given us by the Almighty Creator, to live our lives the best way we can to show forth His praise and glory. Some people have managed to live up to this responsibility despite the avalanche of challenges and difficulties they had to contend with on their journey. One of such persons I am privileged to testify about is the author of this book, Fanella Christiana Sampson.

From the day I met Auntie Fanella, as we affectionately call her, one thing has been obvious in her life: her strong faith in the Almighty God. She is truly a woman of faith, not just in her confessions but more so in her actions and expressions. It will not take you long after hanging out with her to know that her depth of faith has been honed through the experiences of pain, heartbreak, disappointment, and a determination not to give up on the promises of God.

Having had to deal with the tragic and sudden loss of her first husband, becoming a single mother left to fend for herself and take care of her young daughters alone, seeking asylum in a foreign country, fighting almost a two decade immigration battle, facing the affliction of losing yet again a second husband, and all the unfathomable health battles in between, one will wonder how she manages to still keep going and growing stronger.

I cannot even begin to tell you about the generous and the unrelenting hospitable heart that Fanella embodies. Even in her pain, she always finds a way to do something for the well-being of others. My family and I have been personal benefactors of her kind-heartedness. All these and many more she willingly did and continues to do out of the abundance of her love and faith in her Lord and Savior, Jesus Christ. As the scriptures intimate, "they overcame him by the blood of the lamb and by the word of their testimony" (Rev 12:11).

Therefore, as you familiarize yourself with her testimony, it will become for you, a source of strength and encouragement for your own journey of faith. No man, they say, is an island; and iron sharpens iron. I am very optimistic that Fanella's testimony will touch you at whatever stage of life you find yourself, minister to your heart about the faithfulness of God, and also challenge you to live your best life, in the face of life's struggles and trials, to the glory and praise of your Maker and Savior Jesus Christ.

Pastor Wonder Abodakpi, Hope International Ministries, Tulsa Oklahoma

PREFACE

The purpose of writing this book is to share my life experiences and to showcase how God has seen me through all my life's journey. I'm especially grateful that I am in 2020, the year of my seventy-second birthday. I give Him all the GLORY!

Psalm 90:12 says:

"So teach us to number our days, that we may apply our hearts unto wisdom"

As in, teach us to consider, contemplate and meditate upon the winding circuit of the life that you, Lord, apportion to us. So that we may obtain wisdom thereby and be a living instruction to ourselves and also to others.

Oftentimes, wisdom can be an acquired taste; as in, we don't immediately realize or appreciate its value or even its existence in our lives. Sometimes it is like old wine, whose flavor must ripen over time to fully produce its value.

Such has been the nature, tenor, texture and journey of my life. Looking back, although I have constantly given God thanks and the glory along the way, it is only now --that I have become like the wine which is truly ripened and aged to perfect aromatic flavor and quality --that I can truly, more importantly, fully give God the glory and use my own experiences as a testimony and a guide to help others.

May these words be a blessing to all who read if they read in faith and with a mind to know the truth of God through our Lord and Savior Jesus Christ. Amen.

Fanella Sampson
January, 2020

*And he said unto me, Write: for these words are true
and faithful (Revelation 21:5)*

Lumbering among the rye
Its wavy and sanguine rustle
At length did my eye espy
Her for whom is this hustle

Her gait and her manner
Intent and supplicative
Hoisted no small banner
Her plea so evocative

A woman of faith and purity
Her God will not despise
His Word is not a nullity
Great wonders will abide

We thank God for you, Fanella
We thank Him so very much
Yours is a Divine novella
True Grace of God is such

-the poet, 2018

Chapter One

FEARFULLY AND WONDERFULLY MADE

(Psalm 139:14)

My name is Fanella Christiana Tucker. I was born on Friday, May 21, 1948 in Pepel, Freetown, Sierra Leone in West Africa. I am fluent in Creole or Krio, an English-based creole language (which is spoken by 87% of Sierra Leone's population), Mende (which is spoken by 31 % of the population) and English (which is the official language that was brought to the country by its former colonizers).

I have three children: Estella, Osmunda and Minella. I've been blessed with seven grandchildren Syerra, Mariama, Sariah, Rashid, Kyndall, Todd III (Tre') and Mahalia.

My mother, Mariama (Maria) Kamara, was Temne by tribe, a Muslim, and was a fishmonger by trade. My mother as I was told, had many children before me but because of witchcraft in the village she would always loose them through sickness and untimely death. My mother told me that my birth was peculiar, because when I was born my hair appeared to be in braids/locks. As a result, nobody was allowed to take care of me or touch my hair except her. She said if someone else besides her did so, I would break my neck, (lack of muscle strength in neck). I was always puzzled about my hair appearing in braids/locks at birth. My mind often went to Samson in the Bible who had braids and locks in his hair (Judges 16:13, 19). As I reflect on it now, it amuses me to picture a baby with a head of hair like that!

Eventually the locks went away and my hair grew as it normally would. My new hair growth was also a phenomenon to people. They would often argue about if it was real or fake.

My mother was blessed with 3 children after me. Francis, Cyril, and Imma. Francis went to Nigeria to work and would send letters occasionally. But after a while we lost communication. It's been over thirty years now.

Cyril has eleven children and currently lives in Freetown. My sister, Imma, who lives in Virginia, USA, had six children. One passed away and she now has five living children. I only got to know of my sister's existence very late. She was in her teens when we were introduced. She was not given the opportunity to go to school until I met her.

I was very blessed by Mr. and Mrs. Francis Seilenga, (may their souls rest in peace) who helped me put Imma in school. She'd been living with them in Bo, a village in the Southern Province of Sierra Leone. After passing her Common Entrance exams she moved to Freetown to live with me. I enrolled her into a high school just a few steps from where I lived on Fort Street.

While my kid sister Imma stayed with me, she became romantically involved with my neighbor's son and got pregnant. I didn't know about their relationship until after I'd found out she was pregnant. There developed a big feud between me, my sister, and the young man's family because they wanted an easy way out. I stood my grounds and said, "NO ABORTION". They finally accepted and she had a bouncy baby boy. Years later, an aunt brought the young boy to the United States and gave him the best education. He Is an engineer and works for the U.S. Navy and is presently deployed overseas. In the fullness of time, the child my sister wanted to abort ended up bringing her to the United States where she now lives. Praise God!

In the book of Romans 11:33, the great Apostle Paul choruses the age-old adage:

"O the depth of the riches both of the wisdom and knowledge of God! How unsearchable are his judgments, and his ways past finding out!"

Oftentimes the strangest of beginnings are a precursor to the most unlikely and eventful outcomes.

I recall the story of baby Moses in the Bible, born in a time of great spiritual upheaval and widespread death and destruction of innocent lives of Hebrew children in the land of Egypt (Exodus 1:15-22). Nobody would've thought the baby Moses would survive in those circumstances —and through the most unlikely and uncanny of circumstances: his parents placing him in a small patchwork raft on the river and allowing the hand of Destiny and Providence to guide his future and purpose downstream and ultimately into the arms of Pharaoh's daughter.

Subsequently, Moses would be raised in the safest place in all of Egypt: the house of his mortal enemy, the representative of Satan himself in the land, entangled and intermingled —by default --with all the satanic trappings, dark forces and elemental influencers and customs of the pagan and idol-worshipping Egyptian peoples. Not the place you would expect the Grace of our God to thrive or a chosen route for the manifestation of God's salvation, glory and praise. But that is God's way. That is His paradigm: out from darkness comes the light; "how unsearchable are his judgments, and his ways past finding out."

Again, I can only give God the glory for His wisdom

as I marvel at the circumstances and situation of my own birth amid so much death, and the dearth of hope and optimism about my own survivability and future. The uncanny ways in which He orchestrated my deliverance, growth and development from childhood into adulthood would be replayed over and over throughout my adult life revealing the unmistakable, signature Hand of the Divine in the evolution and manifestation of my life's purpose and that of my children and grand-children.

We also see in the story of Joseph, a child stolen from his parents and sold into slavery in Egypt, later being framed and thrown into Pharaoh's prison –surely, his future and prospects eclipsed and imperiled by the cruel hands of fate? Yet, it is this same Joseph that in the fullness of time was elevated to the premiership of Egypt and became the savior of his family and his nation: "how unsearchable are his judgments, and his ways past finding out." I see this paradigm played out in the 'unwanted' child of my sister Imma, whose life was almost extinguished by abortion, but in due course becoming the vehicle God would use to usher his mother into a better future in the United States.

Proverbs 3:5-6 says:

"Trust in the Lord with all your heart, and lean not on your own understanding; in all your ways acknowledge Him, And He shall direct your paths."

Chapter Two

HEMMED IN AROUND
AND ABOUT ME
(Psalm 139:5)

My father, Cecil Tucker was a Sherbro/Mende by tribe. He worked at the Public Works Department (PWD) as a 'turner' (a special skill set) in Bo. He had a brother by the name of Momodu and a sister Fanella (who I was named after). My father was an alcoholic but was knowledgeable in his work skills, so much that if he didn't show up for work, the company will send people to go looking for him. He was very good with his hands and a great asset to the company. I never saw my dad go to church except on my wedding day.

As I've now mentioned them by name, perhaps this is a good spot for a little digression for some background about my people, the Shebro/Mende.

As I mentioned already, oftentimes the strangest of beginnings are a precursor to the most unlikely and eventful outcomes. This is certainly true of my ancestral tribe the Shebro.

As I said before, my tribe's economy and trade is based on fishing. This has been our ancestral pastime and occupation for generations, alongside trading by boat with neighboring people in villages along the coast. In the 17 Century Portuguese, Spanish and Dutch explorers and traders traversed this area intermingling with the Sherbro and other tribes up the river (then referred to as the Madrebombo River in Spanish).

In time however, this trade morphed under different charters and auspices into a nexus for slavery in West Africa, with Sherbro Island developing into a major slave exporting outpost to the Americas.

After the British Crown government abolished slavery in 1808 in cooperation with the United States, it used the erstwhile trading outpost on Sherbro Island as a base to coordinate naval policing activities against illegal slave traders and liberated slaves were ultimately resettled in the Freetown, later to become

Sierra Leone's capital. Another example of darkness giving way to the light and God's redemptive purpose of deliverance and the equalization of opportunities through Christian thought and practice becoming overlaid and entrenched over what was once a blanket of darkness and despair.

Sherbro Island –also known as Bonthe island – experienced a radical in demographic as waves of freed slaves from the British Empire and the Americas populated the area and set up new communities and trade throughout the 19th century. Even as late as the 1970s trade thrived in this area with a vibrant social life almost rivalling Sierra Leone's then rapidly growing capital Freetown.

But as Freetown expanded and evolved and businesses gradually migrated to the mainland, Bonthe eventually lost its glow and shine as a premier trading town. However, the island's past is never far away as old glory days are littered in the oft-dilapidated remains of Bonthe's history, which lines its sandy streets. God's purpose has been in evidence here and will continue to be in evidence through the Divine manifestation of His will for this historic tribe and her people. Amen.

My great grandfather, Moinama Massaquoi, had eight children. Elizabeth (my father's mother) was the first born. Grandma Elizabeth had three children, Cecil, Momodu and Fanella. She was a petty trader and had a shop attached to her house where she did her trading. She baked bread and buns (cookies). She also taught me how to make soap and we would go out on Saturdays to the nearby villages to sell.

Looking back on these humble times, there are precious values to draw from them. The value of being hard-working and economical with what you have, and learning how to stretch a resource from one inch to go one mile. Throughout my life I have sought to instill these values in my children and grandchildren.

Proverbs 18:9 says:

"One who is slack in his work is brother to one who destroys"

Too many today eschew hard work and instead have a sense and attitude of entitlement. This is contrary to good morals and Bible teaching. Even in the work of God, it is very sad to observe and report that this attitude is rife among Believers and even among Ministers of God. They are wasteful, greedy and covetous.

People of God –and especially Ministers of God --do not settle for what is affordable (by the folks in the pews). Rather they place yokes upon their necks to pay for a lifestyle for the Ministers of God, especially, that the people in the pews cannot afford for their own selves. When in fact, the shepherd is supposed to care for the sheep –and then, of course, the sheep will truly love and take care of a loving and dutiful shepherd.

Mark 10:45 says:

"For even the Son of Man did not come to be served, but to serve, and to give His life a ransom for many."

This is the model Christ established and any true servant of His –if, in fact, they are His servant –must exhibit and demonstrate these credentials if we must take them serious as servants of Christ.

Molly was the second born of my great grandfather. She had two children, Amadu and Comfort. She was very popular in our community for her culinary skills. In her adult life, she worked in the role of Inspector for the Bo Town Market and was also a Sunday school teacher at the United Methodist Church (UMC). She was the backbone of the family, accommodated all, and was always ready to help anyone in need.

There are always people like Grandma Elizabeth and Grandma Molly planted by God in a family to allow Him a vehicle by whom He might unfold and manifest His working salvation.

In Genesis 37:22, 26 & 29, we see that Reuben and Judah were just such persons among Joseph's brethren –particularly Reuben, whose desire, ultimately, is that he might free Joseph and deliver him from the other brothers' evil plans. However, we see that Reuben was thwarted because in this instance it was actually God's hidden plan that Joseph go through his ordeal in order that God might perfect, train and mature Joseph for the very important assignment He would charge him with much later in life.

"And Reuben said to them, "Shed no blood; throw him into this pit here in the wilderness, but do not lay a hand on him"—that he might rescue him out of their hand to restore him to his father… When Reuben returned to the pit and saw that Joseph was not in the pit, he tore his clothes" (Genesis 37:22, 29)

My great grandfather had twins, Taiwo and Gina. Taiwo had two children, Hannah and Doniclo. Gina, had twelve kids but only Joe, Christian, Teneh and Yattah are alive today. Ginnia (Gbassay), Moidubor, Umu, and John were the other four that made up the eight kids that my great grandfather had. A big family but the two grandparents that where influential in my life were Grandma Elizabeth and Grandma Molly.

Chapter Three

THE CITY THAT CANNOT BE HIDDEN
(Matthew 5:14)

At an early age, my paternal grandmother, Elizabeth Massaquoi-Tucker, came and took me away from my mother to an Island called Bonthe, where she lived.

Bonthe is a district of Sierra Leone with capital in the town of Mattru Jong, and Bonthe is the largest city where I lived with Grandma Elizabeth on Sherbro Island. As of the 2015 census, the district had a population of 200,730. Bonthe District is one of the sixteen districts of Sierra Leone, itself subdivided into eleven chiefdoms.

The District occupies a total area of 3,468 km, borders the Atlantic Ocean to the west, Moyamba District to the northwest, Bo District to the southeast and Pujehun District to the south.

Bonthe District owns one of the world's largest deposits of titanium ore (rutile) in the world. Sierra Rutile Limited, owned by a consortium of US and European investors, began commercial mining operations in Bonthe in early 1979. However, a variety of institutional setbacks have intervened to deny the region the benefits of this immense economic potential.

I remember the tropical Island as a peaceful place filled with coconut trees, palm trees and mango trees. It was also known for its agriculture in swamp rice. Needless to say fishing was a daily norm and the Island was known for its variety of fish such as grouper, mackerel, jack and barracuda. I used to look forward to when the fishermen will get back inland and we got to savor the catch of the day. Grandma Elizabeth could also throw down in the kitchen, but nothing compared to what her Sister Molly could do.

Cassava was a vegetable that was another staple food. Used in various forms: we would boil it or grate the cassava and make into foofoo or garri. The leaves of the cassava are used to make plasas (a sauce that you eat with rice).

Bonthe and the nearby towns are rich in many things, one of which is the abundance of palm trees. The palm tree is used to produce many things like palm wine (a sap that is collected by cutting the top of the palm trunk and drilling a hole into the trunk to produce the palm wine). We also get palm oil from the fruits of these trees and another type of oil from the nut called palm kernel oil. The palm oil has various benefits. Some of them Grandma Elizabeth showed to me.

As I mentioned earlier, she showed me how to make soap, which was done using the palm oil. We would use the leaves of the palm tree to make mattresses by drying them out and stuffing them in bags, and the veins of the leaves' branches we used to make brooms.

It is interesting how we used everything around us for food and also to make household accessories in the manners I have described. Again, the lessons learnt and gleaned from these early childhood experiences were that nothing is to be wasted. But everything that God has provided is to be used to the full in thanksgiving to a benevolent and gracious Creator.

Once more, my mind is cast back to the historic significance of Bonthe, the veritable and antiquated Atlantic seaport in southwestern Sierra Leone, which lay on the eastern shore of Sherbro Island atop the Sherbro River estuary. This 19th-century British control post against the slave trade, and later settled by freed African slaves, grew in importance as a shipping port for agricultural products. Even today, its harbor still exports palm kernels, ginger, cassava and coffee. However, the silting up of the estuary, coastal swamps, and new internal routes have somewhat degraded and diminished its long-term importance as a commercial seaport.

Sierra Leone as a whole, besides the Sherbro Island region, has a terrain and soil type of the lateritic kind; its weathered and leached formations rich in oxides of iron and aluminum and of a rust-colored texture. Historically, in cosmopolitan cultures of near-antiquity, ruins often disclose laterite as having been used as a building component in cisterns, sewers, headwalls, culverts, and flagstones for generations. Even today, Lateritic soils remain some of the best natural ingredients for use in compressed earth bricks, because of their rich composition of cohesive silt and clay.

The metaphor here is striking and unmistakable: that God in His infinite wisdom allowed the weather-beaten and leached peoples of Sierra Leone through years of historical conflict, pain and struggle to come to grips with their own natural beauty and potential in a uniquely, West African blend of exotic cultures combining 16 ethnic groups and 23 distinct languages within the country. This is also a land rich In diamond and other highly sought-after mineral deposits. Sierra Leone and its outlying and composite districts and provinces is a truly blessed nation. A city that cannot be hidden.

Chapter Four

THE LATTER SHALL EXCEED THE FORMER
(Haggai 2:9)

So, on Fridays and Saturday's in Bonthe, the town hosted a fair and everyone would bring their merchandise to market and sell. This was a great time to socialize with everyone. As a young girl, it was an event I looked forward to as I was free to roam, play and have loads of fun with the other kids. We were a close-knit community.

My grandmother, Elizabeth, loved Bonthe and she was happy to have me living with her. Grandma Elizabeth dedicated herself to the teachings of Christianity and made me her disciple and pupil in the things and the worship of Christ. My mother used to put strings of stuff on my neck and waist for 'protection'. But Grandma Elizabeth, a very strong believer in Christ, upon seeing all that ornamentation on me, took them all off when we arrived in Bonthe. I vividly remember her throwing them away and remarking that she didn't believe in those native superstitions. These trinkets, as I later found out in my teenage years, usually had charms and dark powers tied and attached to them. Grandma Elizabeth spent time teaching me about Christ and she instilled in me the importance of worship and prayer.

Aunt Fanella (dad's sister), had been married for a long time without having children. In time, Grandma Elizabeth took me to live with her. My aunt's husband was a well-known businessman (Mr. Kpange). He was of the Roman Catholic faith and so I was enrolled into a Catholic school. While staying with them, my aunt finally had a baby girl. Unfortunately, due to her drinking habit, she didn't last long in her marriage. I was sent back to live with Grandma Elizabeth when her marriage to Mr. Kpange ended.

Grandma Elizabeth enrolled me in the Minnie Mull Memorial School, a missionary elementary school for girls. I did not come from a rich family. We were poor.

Grandma Elizabeth would modify her skirts into clothes I could choose from and wear to church. Thank God we had to wear uniforms to school. She would buy handmade slippers made from old car tires for me. We used ashes and salt to brush our teeth, and chopsticks were used as toothbrushes. I would walk miles to and from school every day. Sometimes, I would go crab fishing by the river next to our house and gather empty bottles from the riverbank to sell so that I could help make money to get the bare necessities.

Zechariah 4:10 says:

"For who hath despised the day of small things? For they shall rejoice and shall see the plummet in the hand of Zerubbabel with those seven; they are the eyes of the LORD, which run to and fro through the whole earth."

And Job 8:7 says:

"Though thy beginning was small, yet thy latter end should greatly increase"

Just because we begin a certain way, doesn't mean we will end that way. God has a plan for everyone. The key is seeking and holding onto Him for the revelation or ultimate unveiling of that plan in our lives. With perseverance and faith –and obedience to His will –we can overcome our challenges so that His name is glorified.

My school mates were from middle class or rich families, but I was never envious of their wealth. I had a very dear friend who would always bring extra things for me to use. I stayed humbled and always had faith that God will provide. God has always been faithful. He always made a way through His chosen divine helpers.

Grandma Elizabeth made sure I stayed in school, as that was an avenue to a better tomorrow. I was a diligent and God-fearing student growing into a young woman. I didn't allow anyone or anything to take me off my course. The words of my grandmother were always at play in the back of my mind, which were that "God wants nothing but the best for us", and "if we remain obedient and focused that a better day will surely come".

After the death of my grandfather (Pa Tucker), my grandmother had a relationship with Pa Charles Farkeh. Since she wasn't of childbearing age, Pa Farkeh, wanted another wife who could bear him children. So, he talked to my grandmother to arrange with a younger woman to marry him. This was done and Pa Farkeh promised my grandmother that when they would be blessed with a child, he would let her raise the child.

In 1947, the new wife Louisa, gave birth to a premature baby girl who was named Elizabeth after my grandmother and she raised her as her own. The child Elizabeth never knew of her biological mother (Louisa) until later in life. My grandmother and Pa Farkeh built a house in Bonthe on 14 King Street and Palm Street junction. The section in Bonthe was called Nyorgoihun (Sugar Cane). I haven't visited Bonthe for over fifty years, but I've been told that the family house is still standing.

My grandmother was left in the house while Pa Farkeh and his young wife went to Kono (which is located in the eastern part of Freetown) to work at NDMC until his retirement. They had seven children: Elizabeth, Nancy, Augusta, Baby Ann, Rebecca, Darling and James who was nicknamed by my grandmother (*man na hous*) since he was the only boy in the house. Only Elizabeth, Baby Ann and James are living.

Chapter Five

FOLLOWING THE LIGHT
(John 8:12)

As I grew older, I began to notice that I had some unusual abilities. I didn't understand at the time what was going on in my life. At a young age I could see things other people couldn't see.

We would cook outside and in the mornings I would have to sweep the kitchen before going to school. Some mornings I will find juju stuff (just like the ones my mother used to put on me) in my grandmother's fireplace and I would throw them away. I never told my grandmother because I knew those where things she despised. So, every time I found them, I would toss them out. I was always scared to go outside early in the mornings, especially if dogs in the neighborhood were barking. Because when I went, I would always see images dressed in white and any house that those images go into, someone from that house will die few days later. This ability that I had at such a young age scared me, so I kept it to myself. I also noticed that I would have visions and whatever I saw would come to pass.

In the Scriptures, we are instructed to put away from us the accursed thing, because of the negative influences and effects they have on us as they prevent us from receiving the grace and benefits of God's salvation and mercies.

In Joshua 7:1-23, we see how Achan's appetite for the unclean and accursed things brought bad luck and misfortune to the entire nation of Israel. This is how and why some families suffer; because someone is dabbling in things which are accursed and that defile the flesh and the spirit.

Joshua 7:10-12

"And the LORD said unto Joshua, Get thee up; wherefore liest thou thus upon thy face? Israel hath sinned, and they have also transgressed my covenant which I commanded them: for they have even taken of the accursed thing, and have also stolen, and dissembled also, and they have put it even among their own stuff. Therefore the children of Israel could not stand before their enemies, but turned their backs before their enemies, because they were accursed: neither will I be with you any more, except ye destroy

the accursed from among you"

At both my grandparents' houses, we always entertained strangers. They often let me know that it is a good thing to do because you will never know when an angel will visit.

Hebrews 13:2 confirms that this is a Biblical injunction:

"Be not forgetful to entertain strangers: for thereby some have entertained angels unawares"

There was always leftover food in the house just in case someone visited. More importantly they taught me the value of being kind, regardless. They were devoted to sharing and during the holiday time they will go all out to cook and give to neighbors. This became a tradition and it is one that I practice to this day. They instilled in me the significance of being charitable to everyone regardless if we knew them or not.

My grandmother, Elizabeth went to church, rain or shine (very dedicated just like her great granddaughter Estella). She served in the church and would go clean the church on Saturdays. She was a very faithful worshiper with strong faith. My daughter Estella reminds me greatly of her in the way she takes God's work seriously. When I now listen to Estella sing or preach things that were dear to my grandmother, I'm taken back to precious moments we shared.

We were poor but my grandmother's faith in God always saw us through. Days when we didn't have anything to eat at the house, she would always ask us to kneel down with her in her bedroom and we would pray together. Sometimes by the time we finished praying, someone would be at our door with either food or money to give us. That's how strong her faith was, and I learned a lot by trusting God for all my needs especially growing up in such environment.

Despite all the challenges growing up, I finished elementary school at Minnie Mull Memorial School in Bonthe and went to High school at Centennial Secondary in Mattru Jong and Bumpe High School respectively.

In my final year in High School, I was a senior prefect of the school. I met Nat Bangura at this time when he came to do teaching practice from Njala University College. I was not interested, but my girlfriends talked me into giving him a chance.

After High School, my grandmother asked me what I would like to do next since they couldn't afford for me to go to college. I told them that I wanted to work in an office as a secretary. My grandmother's sister, late Molly Massaquoi, (may her soul rest in peace) helped me to enroll at a commercial school called Sonnies' Commercial Institute in Bo, Sierra Leone.

While studying at the Institute, I lived with Grandma Elizabeth's sister Molly, who also was very strong in her Christian faith. She would wake us up at 5:00 a.m. every morning for devotions, singing (even though she didn't really have a singing voice), reading of the bible and prayers before anyone left the house each day. On Sundays, if you didn't go to church you would enter her 'black book' for the whole week. She would be unhappy with you on account of that. Also, she didn't allow us to do any work on Sundays. We did all cooking and laundry on Saturdays. She made it clear to us that Sundays are days to go to church to give thanks to God and a day of rest.

Due to my hard work at the institute, the owner offered me a job to work in his office as a secretary. While there, Peace Corps Office in Bo, Sierra Leone, was looking for a secretary. I was at this time given the opportunity to work at the Peace Corps Office.

One day while at work, Nat, a suitor, came with his family to pay my bride's price (dowry). My family was at first unhappy with my decision because one of my grandmothers, wanted me to be married to another man from our tribe (Mende). Whereas Nat was from the Loko tribe from the Northern Province. Despite the family drama, on Saturday, July 28, 1973, Nat and I were married at the Methodist Church in Bo, Sierra Leone.

My husband Nat Bangura, graduated from Njala University College, BSc(Ed), and taught from 1971-1973.

After teaching, Nat worked as Research Officer and Counterpart Pathologist FAO/IITA in Sierra Leone from 1973 to 1978. My in-laws were unhappy with me at this time, because I was not yet pregnant. I depended on God alone, so I put my hope in Him and knew that one day He would give me a child.

My faith in God increased and one night I had a vision. Two tall men dressed in white robes appeared and performed a detailed cleansing on me, from the inside out. In my dream I vomited slimming worms into a round white basin. I did not understand this. But after that vision of cleansing, I got pregnant.

At this time, I started seeing a renowned gynecologist by the name of Dr. Peters who diagnosed me with fibroids and started treating me to save my baby. In 1975, my husband was offered a scholarship to do his second degree (MSc) in Oklahoma State University in Stillwater, U.S.A.

When Nat left for the U.S., I went to work for my old High School in Bumpe. While he was in the States, I gave birth to a bouncy baby girl on Easter Sunday, March 30, 1975. Three months after her birth, I left her with her paternal grandmother, Aie Warren Bangura in Gbendembu, Sierra Leone to join my husband in the United States of America.

Chapter Six

ETERNAL, IMMORTAL, INVISIBLE, ONLY WISE GOD
(1 Timothy 1:17)

I arrived in America and lived with Mr. and Mrs Bai Kamara in Tulsa, Oklahoma while my husband was doing his course in Oklahoma State University in Stillwater. While in Tulsa, I enrolled at Draughon School of Business going to school at night while working during the day to pay for my education, biweekly. After my husband's graduation, he left me and went back to Sierra Leone while I stayed to finish my course. After my graduation, I left for Sierra Leone as well.

Back in Sierra Leone I was again employed by Peace Corps office in Freetown. While working there, my husband was given a diplomatic job in Monrovia, Liberia at WARDA from 1978 - 1983. I left and joined him but later became tired of being a housewife, so while pregnant with our second child I came back to Freetown, Sierra Leone.

I gave birth to my second child, a bouncy baby girl on December 4, 1979. I continued to work for Peace Corps, got pregnant again with my third child and gave birth to another baby girl on October 9, 1983. She wasn't bouncy as she was born premature. My last born Minella, could fit in the palm of your hand. She stayed in the incubator for weeks as she developed. Minella was delivered by cesarean and we were both fighting for our lives. God saw us through as we were able to leave the hospital sooner than expected. At this time my husband was working as an Acting Sub-Regional Coordinator Zone II from May, 1984 through January, 1987.

In 1988 while working for Peace Corps, there was an opening at the American Embassy's USAID office (U.S. Agency for International Development). I was offered this job and took it because it was paying more than the one at the Peace Corps Office. I worked there until August 1990.

Working at the Embassy was very challenging. Applying for a visa to America in those days was not easy. People were not educated about how to go through the process. I was privileged to educate people on visa process and procedures. Some offered me money, but I always refused, because God gave me the heart to help anyone in need. I always remembered my grandparents' still small voice in my ears. They'd always been willing to help or give to anyone in need and expecting nothing in return. I believe in being someone else's angel. So, helping came naturally. It was a way of life for me. Those who were grateful for the help never forgot the kindness I showed to them.

The favor was returned to me years later when I came to the States seriously ill, in 1990. Grateful hearts brought me groceries, and some helped me in their own ways. You will never loose when you are warm hearted and willing to help someone. I grew up being helped by someone, so I have always given back to others. I know how much of an impact that had in my life. Love truly makes the world a better place. I can't fathom what people see in being evil and spreading hatred. My drive is to always show the love of God through acts of kindness to everyone. Regardless if you are kind to me or not.

In Luke 6:38, our Lord said:

"Give, and it shall be given unto you; good measure, pressed down, and shaken together, and running over, shall men give into your bosom. For with the same measure that ye mete withal it shall be measured to you again"

Also, in Acts 20:35, the great Apostle reminds us of

the words of Jesus elsewhere in this way:

"I have shewed you all things, how that so laboring ye ought to support the weak, and to remember the words of the Lord Jesus, how he said, It is more blessed to give than to receive"

Some people only want to receive and not to give. Some feel that by giving to others freely they are robbing themselves of the advantage. The only robbery is of this very selfish group of people, and they are the ones robbing themselves –because, our Lord Jesus is right: it is more blessed, more profitable, more beneficial, to give versus to be on the receiving end. Because God sees your kindness to the needy as a loan unto himself and He will repay big time.

Proverbs 19:17 says:

"He that hath pity upon the poor lendeth unto the LORD; and that which he hath given will he pay him again"

These are the words of God, which are immutable, unchangeable. The only constant in the universe, in a constantly changing world that sits in a perpetual state of flux, disequilibrium and imbalance.

Jesus said of His words:

"Heaven and earth shall pass away, but my words shall not pass away"

This is the same Word that create, forged and crafted the universe:

"In the beginning was the Word, and the Word was

with God, and the Word was God. The same was in the beginning with God. All things were made by him; and without him was not anything made that was made. In him was life; and the life was the light of men. And the light shineth in darkness; and the darkness comprehended it not" (John 1:1-5)

It is astonishing that people will not rather take God's word on many subjects --including the subject of giving --versus the word of a thief and a robber. A lot of church doctrines and general church practice revolves around the premise of the anti-giver; i.e. that person who will not give willingly and freely to help others in need, except to the one person who has made it their agenda to extort and exploit them: the wolf in sheep's clothing, which, sadly, many a Minister of the Gospel has transformed themselves into these days.

"For such are false apostles, deceitful workers, transforming themselves into the apostles of Christ. And no marvel; for Satan himself is transformed into an angel of light. Therefore, it is no great thing if his ministers also be transformed as the ministers of righteousness; whose end shall be according to their works" (2 Corinthians 11:13-15).

Chapter Seven

POWER BELONGS TO GOD
(Psalm 62:11)

In 1990, I had a vision where I saw my heart ripped out by a family member. At the time, I did not take it seriously since it was 'only' a dream. During this same period, one of my husband's sisters went to her village and did some fetish ceremony where she buried a live chicken to harm me. When she came back from the village, she got sick and was hospitalized. Later, she confessed to me what she had done. I also did not take this confession as seriously as I should have.

Until I became seriously ill.

I was so sick that I was hospitalized and went into a coma.

While in this state, I saw myself chained in a vision and was advised not to go back to our house. I also saw a vision where I was told to go to America with my family. When I got out of the coma, I could not talk but was able to write. I wrote the words: "I should be taken to the U.S. but my children should leave first".

My husband did his best and sent two of our girls to the States.

They arrived safely in the States on July 28, 1990. I followed few days later. That is how we ended up in the United States.

The last born, remained in Freetown with her aunt, her father's sister who did not have a child. While with her aunt she was maltreated and abused. My very good friend, Patricia Conteh, took her and cared for her until her paperwork was approved to come to the States.

I arrived in the United States on August 4, 1990, because of medical problems. I'd taken a leave of absence from my job as an Administrative Assistant with the United States Embassy, Freetown, Sierra Leone West Africa where I'd worked since 1979.

While here in the States my husband, Dr. Nathaniel Bangura (Nat), a Plant Pathologist, and Country Liaison Officer for the African Development Foundation (ADF), died of a heart attack in Sierra Leone on April 10, 1992. I was a widow at the age of forty-four.

When I arrived in Washington, D.C. in 1990, I was helped by people that I'd helped long time ago when I worked in the American Embassy in Freetown. They helped me to get an American driver's license. Since I had a driver's license from Freetown, it wasn't a big hassle to get one. All that was required was an eye exam and I was a legal driver in the States. I was also helped by a Sierra Leonean doctor who had lived in the D.C. area for a very long time. He saw me free of charge and gave me medications free. This was also a blessing from above. I give God all the glory.

After getting medical attention in Washington, I then moved to Tulsa, Oklahoma. In Oklahoma I had many challenges. When my driver's license was about to expire, I went to the driver's license office for renewal, thinking it would be an easy task as my first time. I was given hell, so I went home and told my cousin-in-law about my experience.

That night I had a vision, and, in the morning, I told my cousin-in-law that I was going to a different driver's license's office as was shown to me in the vision. He was in disbelief that I was going back so soon after such an ordeal. But since I know the God that brought me into the country and this God whom I served had told me what to do, I obeyed and left.

Immediately I entered the office, I saw and was ushered to the same lady from the other office that had given me hell the previous day. But while talking with her the manager came from nowhere and told her to issue me the license. That's how I got my second driver's license.   When I came out of the office, I thanked God for His guidance and the grace to obey Him when He leads me.   My cousin-in-law was shocked when I showed him the license.   I was confident because I had it at the back of my mind that since God told me --while in my first coma in Freetown --to come to America, He was going to take care of me.

The last driver's license challenge before getting my green card was when my license was about to expire again, for the 3rd time. For this, too, I had a vision and thereafter did exactly as I'd been told in the vision. In the morning, I told Frank (by now I'd remarried) that I was going with him to his job (another part of the city) so that I can go get my driver's license. He did not argue with me and said, "Okay."

By this time, things have become very strict in obtaining a driver's license. It was required that you either bring a passport, green card or social security card; things had really changed.

As soon we entered through the door of the licensing office, we were welcomed by four people from different sections of the office who offered to help without asking for any form of identification. In about two to five minutes I was issued my new driver's license. We came out praising God because this was truly a miracle. I went back home rejoicing.

As a believer, I am trying to empower people to read my story and the wonderful things God has done in my life. If you put your trust in Him and believe in Him, He will surely lead you on the right path.

Perhaps you are reading this and wondering, "how did she live her life with all these challenges but never wavered?"

Children of God, if your trust Him there is nothing you ask for that He will not give you. He has so much to offer us, all we need is to trust and obey.

In Mark 11:23, our Lord Jesus himself announced:

"For verily I say unto you, That whosoever shall say unto this mountain, Be thou removed, and be thou cast into the sea; and shall not doubt in his heart, but shall believe that those things which he saith shall come to pass; he shall have whatsoever he saith"

That is the word of God; tried, proven, established. Unchangeable God.

Some people will say, especially Africans, that you have 'witch' if you can see things in visions and they come to pass. They also called Jesus Satan on account of His uncanny manifestations (Luke 11:15; Matthew 12:24). We are told that some will be so convinced that the children of God are devils that they will believe themselves to be fulfilling God's will by persecuting them (John 16:2). So, these perceptions are not new.

In John 8:12 Jesus said:

"I am the light of the world: he that followeth me shall not walk in darkness, but shall have the light of life"

We need to follow Jesus, the light of the world. And when we do this, it is He that will lead us in the way of the light of life and out of the darkness. Jesus is now in Heaven, seated and waiting until His enemies are made a footstool for His feet. He administers His awesome power and authority through His angelic ministers and through the Holy Spirit to give us guidance and direction of a spiritual and uncanny nature, so that we may be victorious in life and that He alone, ultimately, may have the glory.

May His magnificent name be glorified forever more.

Amen.

Chapter Eight

IF GOD BE FOR US, WHO CAN BE AGAINST US?

(Romans 8:31)

Since I worked for the American Embassy and my late husband had worked for the American government (African Development Foundation, ADF), headquartered in Washington, D.C., I voluntarily went to the Immigration Service in Oklahoma City on March 15, 1993 to procure information (to see if I could go for Nat's burial since I was here for medical reasons). I wasn't advised of rights: right to counsel, right to apply for asylum, (there was war in Sierra Leone at that time) but was placed in deportation status instead. I was told that I had overstayed and was out of legal status in the United States and two choices were available to me: either I leave the United States on my own or the Immigration Naturalization Services (INS) will deport me.

I was fingerprinted, photographed, given a Warrant for Arrest of Alien, an Order of Release on Recognizance, and my passport was taken. Having worked with the American Embassy for years, I did not expect this to happen. So I contacted family and friends from Sierra Leone in the U.S., who advised me to get a lawyer to help. My sister, Ramzeye (Mustapha) Kamara, got me an out-of-state lawyer by the name of John O'Leary (who is now deceased, may his soul rest in peace.)

The lawyer advised me to challenge the arrest as improvident, and in violation of Service Guidelines as per Orantes-Hernandez v. Meese, 685 F. Supp. 1488 (C.D. Cal, 1988), where rights under the 1980 Refugee Act necessarily require that persons in Service custody be advised of the right to apply for asylum.

Because of my exemplary work history representing U.S. interests in Sierra Leone, he (lawyer O'Leary), wrote to say I deserved better treatment. More to the point, the arrest was tainted and should be rescinded with papers routed to the INS Asylum Office of record to request for my case to be reviewed as a necessity in view of deportability and that my arrest was contested.

On June 3, 1993, I signed Asylum papers with the lawyer in Washington, D.C. On June 14, 1993, these documents were mailed via Federal Express to INS Office in Oklahoma City. On June 15, 1993, one of the Officers at the INS office returned the documents to my lawyer. Subsequent to this time as a fighter and believer in God, I applied for the 1995 Lottery and God being my helper, I was selected. The DV lottery qualified me for a GREEN CARD.

On February 23, 1995, I tendered Form I-485 application on behalf of my children to the INS office in Oklahoma City. It was received and stamped by the INS office.

On April 6, 1995, my application and those of my family were returned to me by the INS office with a notation that they "could not accept my application at this time, because priority case numbers were since not established". In fact, when I rendered the application and they were stamped, there were "DV numbers" available on a current basis for all regions/countries for that month. The U.S. Department of State Visa Service office had previously notified all INS offices and U.S. Consulates of this.

There followed a long battle which involved the Immigration going back on their word, lawyers taking money and doing very little to help, and other personal battles as well. All these I carefully documented with dates. I continued to trust in God who brought us to this country.

Romans 8:28 says:

"And we know that all things work together for good to them that love God, to them who are the called according to his purpose"

What amazing promises, if we can but believe in He who is Faithful and He who is True, even our LORD Jesus Christ. This is a Person who withheld not himself from us but gave himself wholly as a sacrifice and a propitiation for our sins. So that we might inherit His righteousness and glorious potential to succeed in every and all circumstances of life.

2 Corinthians 5:21 says:

"For He made Him who knew no sin to be sin for us, that we might become the righteousness of God in Him"

So, that we might become; so that we might inherit; so that we might appropriate and leverage God's righteousness through Christ: God's excellence, God's grace, God's credit, God's power, God's unimpeachable qualifications for every benefit, every visa, every provision in this life –regardless if men say we are qualified or not. In God, through Christ, we have universal qualification in and to all things good. That is the meaning of that Scripture.

Again, I continued to trust in God who brought us to this country.

On February 18, 1997, I was remarried to Franklin Graves Sampson in Eureka Springs, Arkansas. After our wedding in 1997, I again became seriously ill and fell into a coma for the second time.

The doctors could not figure out what was wrong with me. While in a coma, I again had a vision of being bound in chains. While struggling to get out of the chains, in the physical, as I was told by the nurses (while I visibly struggled), I was calling out my daughter's name, Minella, who was still in Freetown, Sierra Leone during the civil war in 1991-2002.

When Frank came to the hospital, they asked him who was Minella and he told them that she is my daughter. I finally came out of it through fervent prayers. My brother, Bishop James Farkeh, came from Maryland while I was in the coma and prayed over me and told Frank that I was going to be okay. I could hear his voice while I was on life support. With God's healing power, I was able to emerge from this second coma as well. I had many challenges in this marriage because we were coming together as a blended family. Frank had children from previous relationships. But I never gave up.

My struggles to obtain legal status in the U.S. continued. I had an appointment with another lawyer in Oklahoma City. Before going for the appointment, I had a vision of the lawyer whom I was going to see for the first time. Going into the appointment, all that I had seen in the vision came to pass (same height, outfit, etc.). I was also introduced to his assistant who took over the case.

On February 19, 2007 this new lawyer filed a Motion to Join with Joint Motion on our behalf to Dallas, Texas. She also requested on November 01, 2007 in her appeal on our behalf for leniency and that the Service Join in our Motion to reopen and remand proceedings. I believe that God brought her into the situation. "Never lose hope. Just when you think it's over God will send a miracle." I was grateful to God for bringing her my way. My faith was increased when I met this lawyer since she was a God-fearing woman.

There is almost no work in life as hard as having to wait. And yet God wants us to wait. All motion is easier than calm waiting, and yet we must wait until God fulfils His purpose in His time. I prayed and cried for sixteen years and asked God not to forsake me. And in my final stretch He did not. In fact, He held me up through all those challenges, so I continued to push through, looking onto the prize. "The greatest battles are won when we pray."

Psalm 62:1

"Truly my soul waiteth upon God: from him cometh my salvation"

Although mostly unseen, the Lord is always near to those who believe in Him and trust and depend on Him for the strength to meet the challenges of life. The second lawyer said that it was impossible, but God sent me an angel who proved him wrong.

On Wednesday, June 3, 2009, it came to pass that I received the long-awaited, long fought for GREEN CARD in the mail and it was back dated three years. Glory to God, Hallelujah!!!

On Sunday, June 28, 2009, I had a Thanksgiving Service at Hope International Ministries in Tulsa, Oklahoma to give THANKS to GOD ALMIGHTY for seeing me through. Even my lawyer was in attendance to celebrate with me as I gave thanks to our faithful God.

TO GOD BE THE GLORY FOR THE THINGS HE

HAS DONE!

Isaiah 46:4

"I will be your God throughout your lifetime— until your hair is white with age. I made you, and I will care for you. I will carry you along and save you"

My husband Frank Sampson was standing with me through it all. He drove me to every one of these hearings, stood by my side as a loving husband. Even during the health challenges that I faced as these immigration battles were going on, he stayed a devoted husband. I will never forget his labor of love towards me and my children. Since many of us in the church were immigrants, this was a corporate victory. I encouraged them that what God has done for me He will do the same for them when their time comes. Only believe and remember that prayer is the key to heaven, but faith unlocks the doors.

Chapter Nine

TEN THOUSAND TEACHERS, NOT MANY FATHERS
(1 Corinthians 4:15)

In 2011, I decided to move to Texas to be closer to my children because of health conditions. My husband was dragging his feet but after retiring, he finally gave in and joined me. In November 2011, we bought a house in Aubrey and moved in. While in Texas we used to go to different churches and in 2016, Frank decided to go back to his Catholic Church.

I went with the flow and joined him for some time but quit going after a while because I was not able to kneel comfortably when asked to. My daughter, Estella, found a church and told me that it was different from all churches she had gone to. She was so excited about having found a church home that I decided to join her and see what brought this commitment. I started going with her to Spoken Word Faith Ministries, a Spirit-filled church and it's a decision I haven't regretted. I see why my daughter was excited. The move of God is happening in this ministry and I'm grateful to be a part of the Spoken Word Faith family.

In November of 2016, I had a vision. That morning, I told Frank that I was in a very large gathering of Sierra Leoneans and Ghanaians. I told him that I don't know who is leaving us again because at that time too many people in the community were dying. I was unaware that this was relating to my husband's death, which happened not too long after my vision.

In 2016, my husband, Frank Sampson, made sure that we renewed our wedding vows. Following his wishes, we did so on November 19, 2016. With Thanksgiving on the way, he made sure to invite all our family members to the house for Wedding/Thanksgiving lunch. Some declined but those who could make it did come. We had a very good get-together. He watched TV with his son-in-law till 2:00 a.m. of November 27.

On the morning of November 27, he woke up and helped visitors going back to pack their bags in their vehicles. My daughter stopped by to pick me up for church and since I wasn't ready, she left and went to church without me. Before Estella left, Frank asked for prayers to be rendered for us since we couldn't make it to church. I went to bed and he did too.

After a while, I saw him sitting on the bed, so I asked him what was wrong. He did not say anything but seeing his demeanor I sensed something wasn't right. I suggested that we go to the emergency as we always do. He put on his clothes and walked into my car without complaining. By the time we got to the emergency he was not responding. All medical treatment was applied for over an hour, but he never came back to life.

Psalm 147:3 says:

"He heals the brokenhearted and binds up their wounds."

Our Lord is the Great Comforter and Healer. This biblical expression has never been this clear to me until Sunday, November 27, 2016. Continue to rest in peace Frank. Our family was in shock and those travelling back to their various cities were in an even bigger shock. This was a big blow to the community.

Despite dealing with the pain of losing my husband, I was dealt an even bigger blow when his family accused me of killing Frank and demanded an autopsy be performed to establish the cause of death. Since I had a clear conscience, I told them to go ahead and do whatever they want to do but I will not pay for it. They called the funeral home and the funeral home contacted me and I gave them the go ahead to do their investigation. The result came to my house and I did not open it but mailed it to the grandson who paid for it.

I depend on God alone; I put my hope in Him. He alone protects and saves me; He is my defender, and I shall never be defeated.

Psalm 62:5

"My soul, wait thou only upon God; for my expectation is from him"

After the funeral, another challenge.

His family were adamant that Frank left a will and I have held onto it. I told them that he did not, but they were never convinced. Since he did not leave a will, I took a probate lawyer.

We, (Frank's children and I) went to court and I was put as administrator for the estate. I give God the Glory because He has given me favor time and time, again. He has done marvelous things for me. When the devil goes hard after you, you go harder and pray. GRACE WINS EVERY TIME. Thanks to all the prayer warriors and my Spoken Word Faith family.

"O Lord, you are my God. I will exalt you; I will praise your name. For you have done wonderful things; your counsels of old are faithfulness and truth" (Isaiah 25:1).

In 2018, while I was planning to do my 70th birthday in May to give thanks to God for being faithful, I had many challenges. Some people didn't expect me to be alive to see my 70th birthday. While preparing I had several health problems, and some wondered if I would make it but through fervent prayers by my church members, family and friends, I went through it. God is still healing his children. He has never failed me. God brought me this far in life so I 100% trusted Him to see me through. They were wondering how I was going to do the celebration. God, my source, provided me with whatever I needed in abundance for the party. Because I trust in HIM, He has never let me down. I always remember my grandmother's still small voice saying to me "PRAY for whatever you want and surely He will provide". God provided and I had a big celebration complete with a thanksgiving church service. To give all glory back to God.

Another challenge in my life was when my daughter, Estella, had problems in her marriage because of following Christ. To my daughter, Estella: "No one has the right to judge you because no one really knows what you have been through. They might have heard the stories, but they didn't feel what you felt in your heart. Not caring about what other people think is the best choice you will ever make. If you can learn from the worst times of your life, you'll be ready to go into the best times of your life. Whatever you do, work heartily as for the Lord not for men" (Colossians 3:23).

"Being honest may not get you a lot of friends but it will always get you the right ones. Sometimes the bad things that happen in our lives put us directly on the path to the best things that will ever happen to us. Pray for the people that pour wisdom into you. That wisdom didn't come without pain. Teach your children that coming home from a failed marriage is better than coming home in a coffin."

I give all glory to God for His continuous protection in my children's lives. I know that my endless prayers will always continue because my God wants nothing but the best for us.

Still standing on HIS promises I am alive and holding up the fort.

Chapter Ten

FIRST THE BLADE,
THEN THE EAR,
THEN THE FULL CORN
IN THE EAR
(Mark 4:28)

I have come to realize in life that no condition is permanent. This was my grandparents' constant reminder to me while growing up. I can certainly attest to that statement.

I went to a wedding of one of my school mate's daughter's in Houston. I met some of our school mates that I had not seen in a very long time. They were amazed to see me in the U.S., and because, for them, time appeared to have stopped for me, being that I hadn't changed much. They, however, had changed quite a bit and were unrecognizable. I could not even remember their names.

Isn't it wonderful how God can change things around? The Bible says: "The last shall be first, and the first last" (Matt. 20:16). A poor girl from an island seen in this great America?

Coming to this country in those days was a big deal. Only the wealthy could afford it. I wonder what they were thinking at that gathering that day. I had my head up praising God within me for the opportunity to be here. God can change any situation around for the best. Despite losing two husbands, He still has continued to provide for me.

From a young girl from the nondescript backwaters of the Sherbro islands using her grandmother's rags for clothes, now being able to bless people with clothes, accessories, jewelry, and what not. And not only material things, but things of spiritual value and wealth as well, which only God can provide through the instrumentality of the Holy Spirit: peace, comfort, health and happiness. A very poor girl from an Island where she was brought up struggling. Is He not our provider? He is my shepherd I shall not want. Praise God!

My life has been a wonder to many, because my God has been a miracle working God. As my late husband Frank used to say when I get seriously sick: "Don't worry about Fanella, she has nine lives... she will recover soon."

I was in coma in Freetown and came out of it, came to America and had another coma and was again pulled out of it. Praise God! Many health challenges but all for His glory because if I had died, I will not be able to tell my story of His works in my life and how He has seen me through.

Psalm 115:17

"The dead cannot sing praises to the LORD, for they have gone into the silence of the grave"

Psalm 30:9

"What profit is there in my death, if I go down to the pit? Will the dust praise you? Will it tell of your faithfulness?"

Isaiah 38:18

"For the dead cannot praise you; they cannot raise their voices in praise. Those who go down to the grave can no longer hope in your faithfulness"

HALLELUJAH!!!

He has been my shepherd I shall not want. He provides for me, protects me, guides me, leads me and He is my all in all. My God is REAL, REAL IN MY LIFE. HIS LOVE FOR ME IS LIKE PURE GOLD.

Come closer to God and you will experience His love and encounter His presence day in and day out in your life. He is REAL my brothers and sisters in Christ.

Psalm 108:13

"With God we will gain the victory, and He will trample down our enemies."

Coming closer to GOD is the best way we can ever live our lives. Don't let anything undermine your connection with the Lord. When challenges come, turn to Him, and let Him deal with your adversaries. He will work on your behalf and give you the victory!

So my advice to you reading my story is to thank God that you are destined to walk in victory and know that He will deal with enemies that come against you as you trust and rely on HIM and accept His presence in your life.

As an advocate based on my experiences in this country, I advise that since a lot of us come from different parts of the world, we should try and put our houses in order while we are in good health. You might be at an age where you are still working, or you may not. Some people rely solely on their job's group insurance policy. What happens if you are seriously ill or you die? Will your insurance cover your expenses? What if not?

My advice to all, young and old, is to try and get a personal burial insurance. It does not cost that much if you think about it. Some are locked in if one starts early. Another advice is that you have a WILL even if you think you don't have anything. No one knows when God is ready to take you from this earth. We should always be ready and live right with God.

Still basking in God's goodness

In 2019, I was given a surprise 71st birthday party by my church family and children. I have never, ever in my life been given a surprise like that. As a calm calculated woman, I did not go into panic shock but held my head up appreciating this gesture. It is a memory that I will cherish forever. My best friend and sister, Ramzeye was in attendance all the way from Minneapolis. She has been a dear sister to me. I couldn't have asked for a better friend. As a birthday gift my children sent me to London on a three-week vacation in August – praise God.

While in London I didn't enjoy the stay to the fullest as I was battling a cold, but I thank God that I was able to visit another country. I give God the glory for bringing me back safely. The night of my departure, I had a vision about fire. In the morning I told my cousin and we prayed fervently over it. When I got to the airport our prayers were answered because my flight was delayed. The plane that I was supposed to depart with could not fly due to a fire hazard problem, so a different plane was substituted with a later departure time. Prayer saved me and others that were supposed to come on that flight. GLORY!

At the beginning of 2020, my health is improving -- praise God! And I am thankful to God for that and much, much more. I am looking forward to the next path of God's amazing journey for me.

POSTSCRIPT

Oh Lord my God, how great you are in all your ways! In my seventy-two years of existence you haven't failed me. You stood as an eminent force in the face of my storms. And my victories where without a doubt, a testament to how faithful you are to those who put their faith and trust in you.

Being born into a family that didn't have the wherewithal to empower, enrich me and prepare me for the life I and any other young child might desire, wasn't a death sentence. Nor did it necessarily narrow or shrink my odds –except perhaps in the reckoning and perceptions of man. God being God, is the ultimate arranger of destinies. He is the author and finisher of our faith. The draughtsman and architect of our future. We must align ourselves with the one who has the final say in all things. We must reach for Him, more so than for the approval, certitude and attestation of man. He is the enlarger of coasts. The breaker of boundaries. The opener of wombs of promise, mystery and fulfillment.

In Jeremiah 33:3 He told the prophet unblinkingly:

"Call unto me, and I will answer thee, and show thee great and mighty things, which thou knowest not"

With our God all things are possible. The Great Jehovah who parted the Red Sea and brought His chosen people across on dry land –then caused their pursuers to perish in those same waters.

The God that caused water to flow out from a rock. The God that caused the Sun and moon to stand still in their circuit by the word and prayer of Joshua until the children of Israel prevailed against their enemies.

He is the God who specializes in making a way where there was no way. He embraces faith and the attitude that will give Him no rest until he responds from Heaven.

He has encouraged us through several Scriptures to have faith, to have greater faith, and to have more faith –that we might see and experience the glory of God.

Isaiah recognized he is this type of God; i.e. one who can be touched by the feeling and emotion of his people in their times of need and distress. Hence, Isaiah's words in Isaiah 62:1:

"For Zion's sake will I not hold my peace, and for Jerusalem's sake I will not rest, until the righteousness thereof go forth as brightness, and the salvation thereof as a lamp that burneth"

The prophet enjoins us, given his own experiences with this God that loves to be 'bothered' and challenged with problems and prayers of His people, in this way:

"ye that make mention of the LORD, keep not silence, And give him no rest, till he establish, and till he make Jerusalem a praise in the earth" (Isaiah 62:6-7)

He is the God that is more than enough (Almighty God): El-Shaddai

The Most High God: El Elyon

Our Lord and Master: Adonai

The Everlasting One: El Olam

The God who will provide: Jehovah Jireh

The God who will give us peace: Jehovah Shalom

The God who sends angels to fight for us: Jehovah Sabaoth

The God who sanctifies us for himself: Jehovah Mekoddishkem

The God who is our righteousness: Jehovah Tsidkenu

The God who heals us: Jehovah Rapha

The God who is present: Jehovah Shammah

The God who is our shepherd: Jehovah Raah

The God who is our banner: Jehovah Nissi

He is the All-Sufficient God; whose Grace is sufficient for all our needs and challenges –past, present and future --through Jesus Christ our LORD;

i.e. no matter what mistakes you or your forbears made (past) or what mistakes you might make now (present) or later in life (future) – His grace covers all, provided you believe and come to Him in faith and humility. Amen.

As I wrote and reflected upon on my life's journey, I became even more thankful and appreciative that our God is marvelous, and all His ways are splendid. I continue to look up to Him alone to help me through this imperfect world.

Though there were times I thought my story was already complete, our good Father would give me a glimpse that He had more in store for me. Waking up from my last coma I had a revelation that I had work to do for His Kingdom. I awoke with a message that it wasn't my time to die and I must see my youngest daughter established here in the States (at the time she was still in Freetown and my ongoing immigration problem was looming). I was also told that I was to do a work for the Lord. Praise God!

As I approach my seventy-second birthday, I am reminded of this mandate and I look to the Lord to perfect His will in me. In this year 2020, I strive more than ever to do kingdom work. I know that being connected to Spoken Word Faith Ministries is for the fulfillment of my destiny.

My life is not exceptional but with God by my side, my unusual circumstances became a portal for me to see the supernatural hand of God in my life. The decision to gravitate towards His light was a personal decision that I made from a very early age with the help of my grandparents.

I'm forever grateful for the upbringing from Grandma Elizabeth. Her Divinely inspired faith and her devotions that were passed down to me, and from me, to my three daughters.

I see the blessings of His Grace and Mercy in the life of my daughter Estella and my grandchildren Mariama and Rashid.   I especially see the evidence that is undeniably the hand of God in Mariama and Rashid's life because of their bold faith that they exhibit. From the moment of exposure and their personal devotion to God, the Heavens, the Throne of God and angelic messengers have been opened to them through miscellaneous and manifold Divine interactions and conversations. All glory to God.

2 Timothy 1:5-7

"When I call to remembrance the unfeigned faith that is in thee, which dwelt first in thy grandmother Lois, and thy mother Eunice; and I am persuaded that in thee also. Wherefore I put thee in remembrance that thou stir up the gift of God, which is in thee by the putting on of my hands. For God hath not given us the spirit of fear; but of power, and of love, and of a sound mind"

I'd put down my umbrella
--or parasol, in sunny Marbella
Suddenly this guy and his fella
Openly begin their acapella

The rhythm from a faraway Favella
Regaled and told a somber novella
About a tried and tested, 'Tesella'
Who gave all to save one Fanella

Aromatic, strong, and pure as canella
He chased out the dark like a padella
T'was Jesus our own Divine 'bonsela'
Descended from the highest cella

For her miracle He calls her 'Marvella'
For consolation He calls her 'Consuela'
However, her name, again, is Fanella
His healing was hers like the prunella

-the poet, 2019

GLORY TO GOD

IN THE HIGHEST